THE LORD OF THE RINGS

THE TWO TOWERS ™

VISUAL COMPANION

THE LORD OF THE RINGS™

THE TWO TOWERS

VISUAL COMPANION

JUDE FISHER

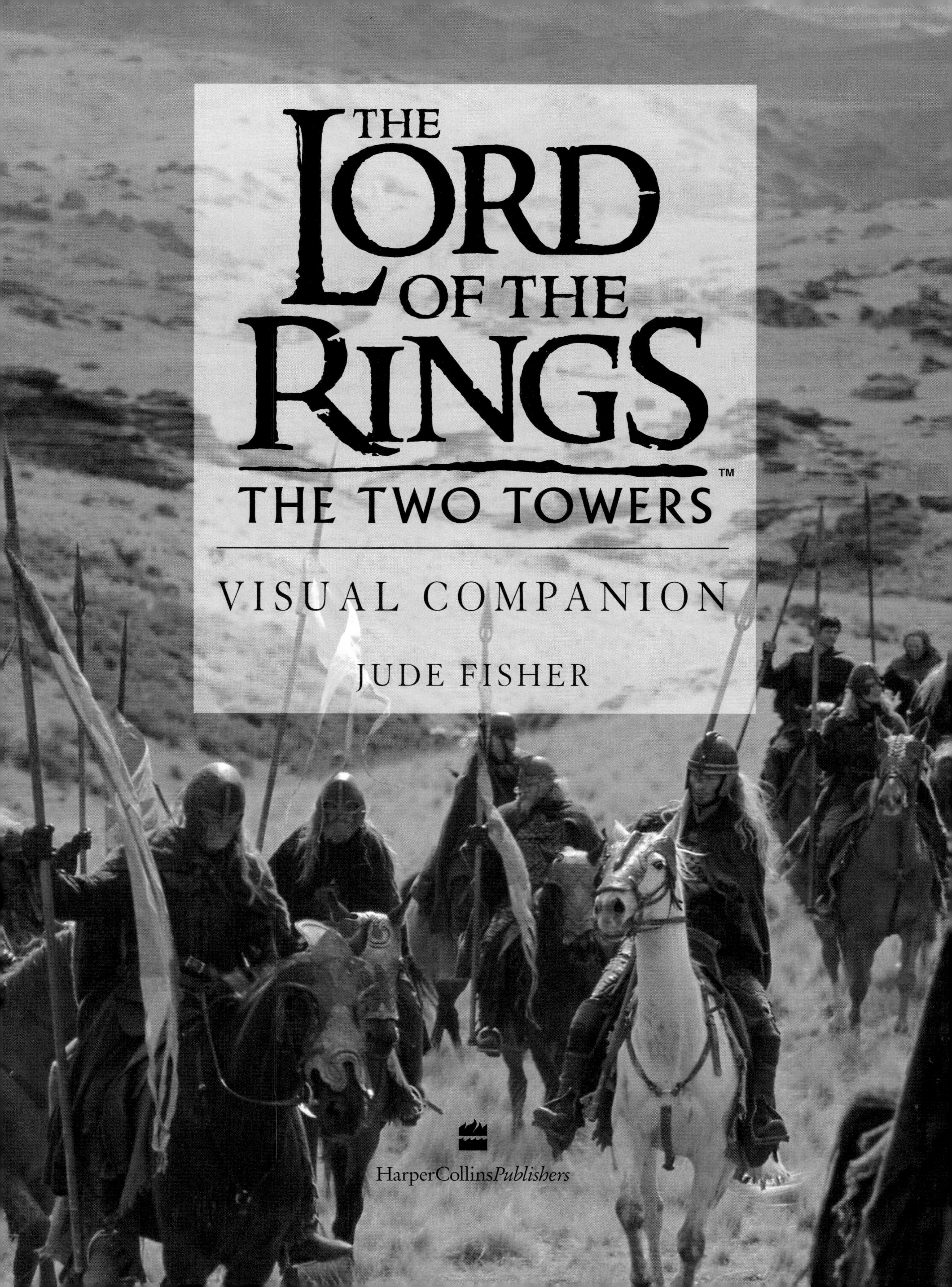

HarperCollins*Publishers*

INTRODUCTION

VIGGO MORTENSEN

Jude Fisher's excellent *Visual Companion* to *The Two Towers* needs an introduction no more than did her equally enlightening *Visual Companion* to *The Fellowship of the Ring*. Since, however, the chance to add a preface has presented itself, it can be hoped that the digression of a few extra words will not do her good work any harm:

The Two Towers, the second part of Peter Jackson's filmed trilogy from JRR Tolkien's heroic romance, *The Lord of the Rings,* comes to theatres in a world that is no more secure than the one in which *The Fellowship of the Ring* was released last year. Tolkien composed his original masterpiece in equally troubled times of terror, war, and uncertainty. The great Nordic poets and saga-writers of medieval Iceland, who provided great inspiration to Tolkien, themselves lived under dictatorship and in times of extreme hardship. It would seem from even a cursory reading of world history that there is no new horror under the sun, that we will perhaps always have to contend with destructive impulses in ourselves and others. That does not prevent us from making an effort to change, from working to find a better way.

"How is it possible that suffering that is neither my own nor of my concern should immediately affect me as though it were my own?"
Schopenhauer

At our best we, like the Fellowship, realize individually and collectively that peaceful co-existence can be achieved only through vigilance and conscious compassion. Compassion for oneself and others, especially for those determined to do us harm. An effort made to identify with others and understand them in order to understand ourselves. To understand that there is no absolute difference between us. That is not to say that we ought to allow ourselves to be trampled, eliminated as individuals, races, or nations. Regardless of the odds faced, it is important to defend oneself and others against oppression. 'It is becoming to be humble, yet at the same time you must make a bold showing if put to a test', as a father advises his departing son in one of the oldest and best-known sagas. The most enlightened beings in Tolkien's Middle-earth are conscious of the ubiquity of good and evil in neighbours, strangers, adversaries and, most importantly, themselves. There can be little future in adopting a permanent policy of 'an eye for an eye'. If we were all regularly to put into effect such an inflexible approach, we would all soon be blind, as Gandhi pointed out. One must pick one's battles and fight only when it is unavoidable.

"Good and ill have not changed since yesteryear; nor are they one thing among Elves and Dwarves and another among Men. It is a man's part to discern them as much in the Golden Wood as in his own house."

Aragorn to Éomer

As JRR Tolkien's story gains momentum and complexity in *The Two Towers*, the situation for the now-fragmented Fellowship and for all well-intentioned peoples of Middle-earth becomes increasingly perilous. Hope has become a flame so feebly flickering that, even to the most stout-hearted and wise, it seems nearly certain to be snuffed out by morning. Even so, Frodo will no more falter in his lonely quest than will Sam in his determination to selflessly assist the Ring-bearer on his arduous journey to Mount Doom. Merry and Pippin, likewise, will continue in their struggle to survive and be of service to their friends and all who would stand against Sauron and his misguided servants. In the isolated reaches of proud Rohan, King Théoden and his brave but vastly outnumbered people will be able to count on the courage of Gimli, Legolas, and Aragorn in their desperate battle against Saruman's terrible army. Gandalf himself will return from seeming oblivion to lend his ageless wisdom and powers of inspiration to the Fellowship and all free peoples of Middle-earth.

5

"He is truly wise who's traveled far and knows the ways of the world. He who has traveled can tell what spirit governs the men he meets."

from Hávamál, as translated by Björn Jónasson

What is unknown, as always, is whether the sacrifices of a brave few can inspire faith in others and, in the end, prove sufficient means to turn the tide and disable the forces that would make slaves of us all. There probably is no such thing as a lasting peace, any more than a garden will ever cease to need weeding and watering. Storytellers and stories change, but the opportunity to do well or ill by others and ourselves will always be present. The right to choose how we co-exist is ours unless we willingly surrender it. There can be no "quick fix", no easy or permanent answer to the troubles of today or tomorrow. A sword is a sword, nothing more. Hope, compassion, and wisdom born of experience are, for Middle-earth as for our world, the mightiest weapons at hand.

"All things are connected like the blood which unites us all. Man did not weave the web of life; he is merely a strand in it. Whatever he does to the web, he does to himself."

Chief Seattle

Namarië!

THE SUNDERING OF THE FELLOWSHIP

"One Ring to rule them all, One Ring to find them
One Ring to bring them all and in the darkness bind them"

The hobbit Frodo Baggins, young nephew of Bilbo Baggins, has inherited a perilous quest: he must prevent the One Ring — an ancient artefact charged with great and sinister power — from returning to its master, the Dark Lord Sauron, by carrying it south and eastwards into Mordor, the Land of Shadow, and there destroy it in the Cracks of Doom, the volcano where it first was made. The Ring, however, has a dark sentience: it wishes always to return to the one who forged it and imbued it with his life-force and his malice; and Sauron's lidless eye ever seeks the Ring. His hordes of Orcs and other monsters roam freely across Middle-earth, bringing annihilation and shadow into the realms of Men, Dwarves and Elves. From his home in the peaceful rural backwater of Hobbiton in the Shire, through Bree to Rivendell, last refuge of the Elves in Middle-earth, Frodo has travelled with the Ring, and there he is joined by a fellowship of companions who volunteer to accompany him on his quest: Aragorn, son of Arathorn; Boromir, son of Denethor of Gondor; Legolas, son of Thranduil, the king of the Mirkwood Elves; Gimli, son of Glóin, a great warrior-Dwarf; the hobbits Meriadoc Brandybuck, Peregrin Took and Samwise Gamgee; and the wizard Gandalf the Grey.

7

But now the Fellowship has been broken. In Khazad-dûm Gandalf was lost in a desperate battle against a Balrog — an ancient fire-demon. At Amon Hen, Boromir fell prey to the corrupt power of the Ring and tried to seize it from Frodo, thinking to use it on behalf of his own people in the war against Sauron, rather than see it destroyed. Aware of the danger of the Ring even to his companions, Frodo then decided to undertake the task by himself; but Sam Gamgee pursued his friend, and the two hobbits set off bravely towards Mordor to complete the quest on their own. Or so they thought; for a strange creature now follows them who would take back the Ring for himself.

The remainder of the Fellowship was beset by a raiding party of Saruman's Uruk-hai, which had been sent to retrieve the Ring and its bearer, and return them to the wizard's strong-hold at Isengard. Instead of capturing Frodo and the Ring, however, they mistakenly carried away the wrong hobbits, Merry and Pippin, though Boromir died valiantly trying to defend them. Thus the Fellowship was sundered and once Boromir's body had been committed to the mercy of the great River Anduin, cast adrift in an elven-boat above the Falls of Rauros, Aragorn, Legolas and Gimli were left with a terrible choice: should they go after Frodo and Sam and join them in the quest to destroy the Ring, or attempt to rescue the two captured hobbits?

After Gandalf's fall into darkness, it was to Aragorn that the leadership of the Fellowship fell, and rightly so, for although he dresses in the worn and simple garments of a Ranger, he is in fact the Lost King of Gondor. Aragorn decided

that rather than abandon Merry and Pippin to certain torture and death, they had to pursue their Uruk-hai captors; leaving Frodo and Sam to make their long, uncertain journey alone.

It is a journey that, as they edge towards the Land of Shadow, will take the two hobbits through harsh landscapes and hostile terrain in which the servants of the Dark Lord are ever present. And with each step that Frodo takes towards the gates of Mordor the Ring, which he wears on a chain around his neck, will feel heavier and more burdensome, dragging him down, ebbing his strength and his will.

On either side of the River Anduin above the Falls of Rauros the country lies in great furrows and ridges cut through with many gullies and ravines. Dark and jagged against the eastern sky run a line of sawtoothed mountains; between the hobbits and these stretch eighty miles of rocky wasteland. It is a borderland known as the Emyn Muil, strewn with ancient ruins, remnants of the great works of Gondor.

Amongst these mist-wrapped cliffs Frodo and Sam finally confront the sneaking figure who has dogged their steps for many days.

GOLLUM

"Slier than a fox and as slippery as a fish"

A lurking presence has dogged the footsteps of the Fellowship since they entered the Mines of Moria, a presence which has been drawn by the evil power of the Ring. This sneaking thing is Gollum; and when Frodo and Sam are separated from their companions amongst the barren, stony slopes of the Emyn Muil they will eventually spy him, spidering around the crags, in search of the Ring.

It is hard to believe, to look at this pale, skinny creature with his long, clinging fingers and toes and his gleaming, bulbous eyes, that once he was a creature not unlike a hobbit. His name then was Sméagol, and he came not from the homely Shire, but was a Stoor, from the lands to the east which border the River Anduin where it runs through the battleground of the Gladden Fields. It was here that Orcs ambushed and overcame Isildur, the King of Men, who carried with him the One Ring which he had cut from the hand of Sauron himself. There the Ring was lost, fallen into the mud at the bottom of the river, and there it lay undisturbed for thousands of years, until the day that Sméagol and his friend Déagol went fishing. Déagol hooked a great fish, which dragged him out of the boat, and when he resurfaced, he had in his hand a golden ring. Sméagol immediately coveted this shiny object; and when Déagol refused to give it to him, Sméagol strangled his friend and stole the Ring away, claiming it as his 'birthday present'.

10

"Everywhere we went the Yellowface watched us until we found a hole and we followed it into the mountain, and in the darkness we forgot the sound of trees, the taste of bread, the softness of the wind ... even our own name"

And thus the Ring began to work its evil influence on the hobbit, making him mutter and gurgle in his throat, so that he became known as 'Gollum'. It caused him to fear the light and the open air, and drove him out of the sight of the sun into the cave system deep beneath the Misty Mountains, where he lived on raw fish and other things that he caught in its lightless pools. There Gollum stayed, alone except for the Ring, which he called his *Precious*, until Bilbo Baggins chanced upon him. Then the Ring, seeking ever to return to the Dark Lord, insinuated itself into Bilbo's possession, and Bilbo carried it away with him to his home in the Shire. Hating the Ring for leaving him thus, and yet loving it all the while, Gollum was forced to leave his dark retreat and come out into the world to pursue his obsession. However, when he emerged from the caves, Gollum was captured by the Dark Lord's servants and brought to the dungeons beneath the tower of Barad-dûr. There he was tortured as Sauron sought to discover the whereabouts of the Ring, but he managed to escape, and has been hunting his Precious ever since.

"No, no, Master! Don't take the Precious to him! He'll eat us all if he gets it, eat all the world"

And so, once Gollum has been 'tamed', caught and bound by the *hithlain* rope that was given to Sam in Lothlórien, Frodo will find himself making a strange alliance: for he and Gollum share the same goal: to prevent the One Ring from falling into the hands of the Dark Lord. Moreover, Frodo needs a guide through the Land of Shadow, and only Gollum knows the secret ways into Mordor.

THE DEAD MARSHES

"Tricksy lights! Candles of corpses! Wicked lights!"

To the east of the Emyn Muil lies a stretch of marshland which in the last three thousand years has crept its way across the battlefield of Dagorlad. This was the site of the last great conflict against the Dark Lord Sauron, in which the Army of Shadow was defeated and he was brought down, heralding in the Third Age of Middle-earth. Led by Gollum, Frodo and Sam must make their way through these stagnant meres without falling prey to the sinister glamour of the dead who may be glimpsed beneath the murky water. Locked in their armour, weeds threading through their silver hair, there appear to lie beneath the surface of the marshes thousands of dead warriors — Men, Elves and Orcs — their faces spectral, their bodies bloated and pale. And all around are ghostly lights — will-o'-the wisps — which, like flickering candles, may tempt the unsuspecting to wander off the safe path, deep into the bog, there to founder and drown.

"You must not look at them when the candles are lit..."

ITHILIEN

In order to avoid direct confrontation with the Dark Lord's army of Orcs, Easterlings and Mûmakil amassing at the Morannon, the Black Gates of Mordor, Frodo, Sam and Gollum must approach their destination indirectly. Heading south, they enter Ithilien, the border country between Gondor and Mordor. This area was originally the land of Isildur, son of Elendil, King of Men, but its proximity to Mordor has resulted in the country long being abandoned by its inhabitants. As the travellers make their way through the climbing woods and upland meadows full of rabbit warrens and wild-flowers, past waterfalls and swift streams, they will come upon the remnants of that once-great civiliza-tion: old roads now unused and overgrown, great statues that have been cast down and crowned with weeds. It is a sad and lovely land, patrolled now only by companies of Rangers who seek to prevent incursions of Orcs and other fell creatures from reaching Gondor.

FARAMIR

Faramir is the second son of Denethor, Steward of Gondor, and the younger brother to Boromir. A stern and commanding man, he is the captain of a band of Rangers who take Frodo and Sam captive as they journey through Ithilien, the border country between Gondor and Mordor. This lovely wooded country is beset by Orcs and other enemies as Sauron's dark forces encroach ever further into the lands of Men. As Captain of the Ithilien Rangers it falls to Faramir to patrol this dangerous borderland and protect Gondor as best he can from these marauding bands, and from the Dark Lord's spies.

"Since the loss of Boromir he does the duty of two sons..."

Even before taking Frodo and Sam captive and learning the truth of the matter, Faramir has suspected the loss of Boromir, his elder brother. Faramir is a sensitive, discerning man, prone to premonitory dreams, and in one such vision he 'saw' the small Elven boat in which Aragorn, Gimli and Legolas had laid their dead companion, floating on the swell of the great River Anduin, and when he awoke he knew in his heart that his brother was dead. This was

16

"for himself ... and the one who will not return."

then confirmed for him some days later when the silver-banded ox-horn Boromir carried as the eldest scion of his house was washed up on the riverbank, cloven in two. It was said of this legendary horn that if it were to be blown anywhere within the ancient boundaries of the realm of Gondor, its call would not go unheeded. But when Boromir fell to Uruk-hai arrows while defending Merry and Pippin, he was beyond the bounds of the ancient kingdom, and the faint echo of the horn was dim and distant.

Their father is Lord Denethor, the Steward of Gondor, one of a long line who has held the kingdom in readiness for the return of Isildur's heir.

Denethor waits in despair for news of his eldest son, despising his younger son all the while, which is a bitter burden for Faramir to bear.

Faramir, like his brother, is tempted to take the Ring to use on behalf of his people. It is among the embattled ruins of the ancient city of Osgiliath that Faramir must decide the fate of the Ring, and its bearer, Frodo Baggins. In his hands lies the future of the Free Peoples of Middle-earth.

MERRY, PIPPIN AND THE URUK-HAI

"Kill all, but not the Halflings... They have some Elvish weapon.

The Master wants it for the war..."

When the Uruk-hai warriors fell upon the Fellowship on the slopes below Amon Hen, Meriadoc Brandybuck and his cousin, Peregrin Took, defended themselves valiantly, even though it was the first time they had borne arms in battle. Aragorn and Gimli fought the Orcish attackers in fierce hand-to-hand combat with sword and axe, and Legolas proved deadly with his Elven longbow; but despite the bravery of the companions the Uruk-hai proved too many and too strong, and the Fellowship was sundered. The fearsome Uruk leader, Lurtz, loosed a rain of arrows which killed Boromir, son of Denethor, and then the ambushers captured Merry and Pippin, recognizing them as belonging to the race of halflings

18

known as hobbits. They had been charged by their master, Saruman the White, with the task of finding a certain hobbit bearing a rare and powerful artefact, and bringing both safely to Isengard: but knowing neither the identity of the hobbit in question, nor the nature of the thing the wizard covets, they mistakenly believe Merry or Pippin is the hobbit they seek.

"We are the fighting Uruk-hai ... the servants of Saruman the Wise, the White Hand..."

Saruman's Uruk-hai have been bred for power, speed and brutality. Great swart, massive-muscled, slant-eyed beasts, they were birthed in the caves beneath the fortress at Isengard, tormented in order to forge their cruel spirits and fed upon unspeakable things. They bear upon them Saruman's mark — a white hand painted on their shields and faces. Tireless and determined, they can run through the day as well as the night, unlike other Orcs, which dislike feeling the sun's eye upon them, and prefer to move in darkness. Their leader — now that the master's greatest creation, Lurtz, lies dead at Aragorn's hand — is Uglúk. Because of their small size, the hobbits are easy to carry so the Uruk-hai make swift progress towards their goal.

FANGORN FOREST

"This forest is old, very old, and full of memory..."

At the southern end of the Misty Mountains there lies a wild and ancient woodland, the remnant of the vast woods that once covered all of this part of the land in the Elder Days. Inside, it may appear dark and forbidding to strangers, full of shadows and strange shapes. Trees stand, rank upon rank, in every direction; some tall and slender and straight, their lithe limbs reaching for the light, while others are gnarled and bent by age, their bark all ridged and scored. Many are clothed in lichen, as if with great beards and whiskers; others are covered in dry brown leaves, and have long-fingered twigs, like hands that may clutch. And sometimes, out of the corner of the eye, it may appear that they have moved not as trees move, with the passing of the wind, but of their own accord. It is an eerie place to travellers who do not know it well; and can be dangerous to those who are not kind to trees. It is not wise to cut live wood to make a camp fire in Fangorn Forest.

"Saruman used to walk in these woods,
but now he has a mind of metal and wheels"

In the south, smoke rises from the factories of Isengard. There, the great Forest has been cut down in swathes: hewn tree stumps mark its ravaged slopes. The wizard Saruman, Chief of the Order of the Istari, who came to Middle-earth to aid the Free Peoples, has been corrupted by his quest for knowledge and power, so that now he thinks to challenge the Dark Lord himself. Driven at first by Sauron's command and lately by his own ambition, he has been systematically destroying the woods that border his fortress at Isengard in order to provide fuel and timber for his many projects of war — fuel for the fires in which dark armour and blades are forged for his great army; timber for siege towers and ladders and battering rams. The trees of Fangorn and their protectors and herds, the mysterious Ents, will not be forgiving of such wanton destruction.

ENTS

"Ere iron was found or tree was hewn,

When young was mountain under moon;

Ere ring was made, or wrought was woe,

It walked the forests long ago."

Inside Fangorn Forest, Merry and Pippin — having escaped their captors — will meet one of Middle-earth's most ancient and extraordinary inhabitants. Because he is as tall as a tree, as gnarled as a tree, as covered in moss and leaves and lichens as any tree, it is easy to mistake him *for* a tree. But Treebeard, or Fangorn (for he shares his name with the forest in which he walks) is a member of the Onodrim, or Ents — guardians and tree-herds to the great forests of Middle-earth.

22

"The oldest living thing that still walks beneath the Sun upon this Middle-earth"

Treebeard is the oldest and wisest of the Ents: for three Ages he has walked Middle-earth, tending the trees and watching the peoples of the world come and go, teaching them the ways of plant and tree and flower.

The name 'Ent' was given to the Onodrim by the people of Rohan, in whose language it means 'giant'; and gigantic they are, standing at fourteen foot and more. They are clad in a substance much like bark, being grey and brown and green and ridged and wrinkled by age. Their fingers are like twigs and their great feet have seven long, gnarled toes that resemble nothing so much as tree-roots. Ents are very slow-moving, and slow-thinking. An Entmoot, or council, can last for days at a time, for Ents like to consider matters carefully; but if at last they are roused to anger, their fury is formidable, and when it is combined with their ancient strength, neither fortress nor army can withstand them. And the Ents of Fangorn will not look kindly upon the ravages of Saruman the White, who has ripped their kin from the land surrounding Isengard root by root, or cut them down where they have for centuries stood in peace.

THE MASTER OF ISENGARD

"The White Wizard is cunning..."

Saruman the White, foremost of the Istari wizards who came to Middle-earth to guide all the Free Peoples against the growing evil of Sauron, Lord of Mordor, has himself developed a great appetite for power in this world. For long years he has studied the ways of the Dark Lord, seeking out arcane knowledge from ancient texts, acquiring magical lore and craft, readying himself to make his move. His stronghold at Isengard, long ago acquired by the wizard as part of his grand scheme, stands in a crucial strategic location: guarding the Gap of Rohan between the White

For in the caverns beneath his stronghold Saruman has created an army of Uruk-hai - Orcs bred with Goblin-Men to make them powerful, cruel and tireless. He has marked them with his own device, that of the White Hand, and these creatures roam freely throughout the lands surrounding Isengard, killing at will.

"...his spies are everywhere"

Having learned from Gandalf the Grey the whereabouts of the One Ring, Saruman is determined to acquire it and use it for his own purposes. He sent an élite band of his Uruk-hai warriors to capture Frodo Baggins, the hobbit Ring-bearer; but when the Uruks set upon the Fellowship beneath Amon Hen, Frodo escaped them and it was Merry and Pippin who were taken captive.

Foiled in this venture, he will launch his monstrous army of Uruk-hai, Wild Men, Orcs, and Wargs upon the Kingdom of Rohan, the country he has weakened from within by the use of his spy and weapon, Gríma Wormtongue, who has poisoned the mind of King Théoden, rendering him incapable of action and decision.

Mountains and the Misty Mountains; and what was once a fortress built to ensure the safety of the Kingdom of Rohan has now become a base from which enemies will issue out to engulf it.

25

THE PALANTÍR

The palantíri are the eight legendary seeing-stones, crystal globes made by the Elves, which could enable a person of strong will to view scenes far away in time and space, especially in the proximity of another seeing-stone. Most have been lost down the ages, but one of the surviving stones fell into the clutches of the Dark Lord Sauron, which made all the other palantíri dangerous to use. Another was housed in Orthanc, where Saruman found it and strove for mastery of it, but this has made him susceptible to the will of Sauron.

THE SHADOW OF SARUMAN

Saruman has established great factories and foundries at Isengard — furnaces and smithies and armouries to forge weapons and armour and engines of war — turning what was once a beautiful landscape of wooded valleys, groves and tumbling streams into a barren wasteland of brambles, sere grass and thorns. Rotting stumps mark the death of trees which have been felled and carried away to fuel his evil fires. Pungent, coloured smoke billows into the skies around Orthanc, poisoning the very air. Saruman's depredations can be seen for miles, a constant reminder to the Ents of the murder done to their wards, the trees, and a warning to the Horse-lords of Rohan of the danger that lurks on their doorstep.

THE PURSUIT

After the conflict below Amon Hen during which the Fellowship of the Ring was sundered, Aragorn made the hard decision that instead of accompanying the Ringbearer and Samwise Gamgee, he, Legolas and Gimli should attempt to catch up with and rescue the missing hobbits, Merry and Pippin, from the marauding band of Uruk-hai that carried them off.

"Some evil gives speed to these creatures and sets its

will against us"

The Uruk-hai which are heading back towards Isengard and their master, the wizard Saruman the White, have been bred for power and speed, and unlike other Orcs have little fear of the light of the sun: the pursuers must somehow track them and run hard for several days and nights across rough terrain if they are to save their friends.

"Where sight fails the earth may bring us rumour.
The land must groan under their hated feet"

Three days and nights' pursuit bring Aragorn, Legolas and Gimli to the Plains of Rohan, where they discover a heap of smouldering Orc and Uruk-hai bodies on the edge of Fangorn Forest, evidence of a slaughter by unknown assailants. But there is no sign of the missing hobbits. Within the Forest, however, there will be a remarkable and unlooked-for reunion.

GANDALF THE WHITE

"I come back to you now, at the turn of the tide."

As the Fellowship, pursued by hordes of Orcs, fled through the Mines of Moria — the ancient kingdom of the Dwarves — a great, distant rumbling was heard; then the ground began to shake and a fierce and fiery light came snaking through the labyrinth of tunnels. The air became hot. A creature of the ancient world had been roused: a fire-demon, a Balrog known as Durin's Bane. Terrified by its presence, the Orcs scattered in their hundreds, swarming up the vast pillars and out across the halls of Khazad-dûm. Shrouded by fire it came, black smoke wreathing about its dark body and horned head. Armed with a flaming sword and a many-thonged whip, it raced towards them.

30

Gandalf the Grey ordered the rest of the Fellowship to save themselves by crossing the narrow bridge across the abyss while he waited in the middle of the span to hold the demon at bay. The Fellowship, looking back from the safety of the Dimrill side of the bridge saw how the Balrog towered above the wizard. They saw the demon's fire answered by the white fire of Gandalf's sword, Glamdring. They saw the wizard strike the bridge with his staff; they saw the span break. They saw how the Balrog, falling, wrapped its whip around the wizard's legs and dragged him down with it into the abyss. And then they saw no more and believed him lost.

But Gandalf did not perish. Down he fell with the Balrog, far below the living earth to the utmost foundations of stone, fighting all the way. When freezing waters

engulfed them the Balrog's fire was quenched, and then Gandalf pursued it through the darkest of tunnels. The demon fled from the wizard, up the secret ways of Khazad-dûm until it reached the Endless Stair which brought the two combatants all the way up to Durin's Tower, carved into the rock of Zirak-zigil. There, where the stair came out at a dizzying height above the mists of the world, the Balrog's fire sprang back to life, and there Gandalf fought him long and hard, so that it appeared that fire and lightning struck the mountain, until at last the fire-demon fell from that high place and found its death.

On that cold mountain, as the stars wheeled overhead, darkness claimed Gandalf. There he lay, lost and stranded, straying out of thought and time. But he did not die, for his task on Middle-earth was not yet done and he was sent back. When Aragorn, Legolas and Gimli search for the lost hobbits in Fangorn Forest, they come upon an old man whom they mistake at first for Saruman, for, under his ragged cloak he is dressed all in white. White, too, is his hair and his beard and his staff. A bright light is in his eye.

Gandalf the Grey is no more; now he has returned, full of power, as Gandalf the White.

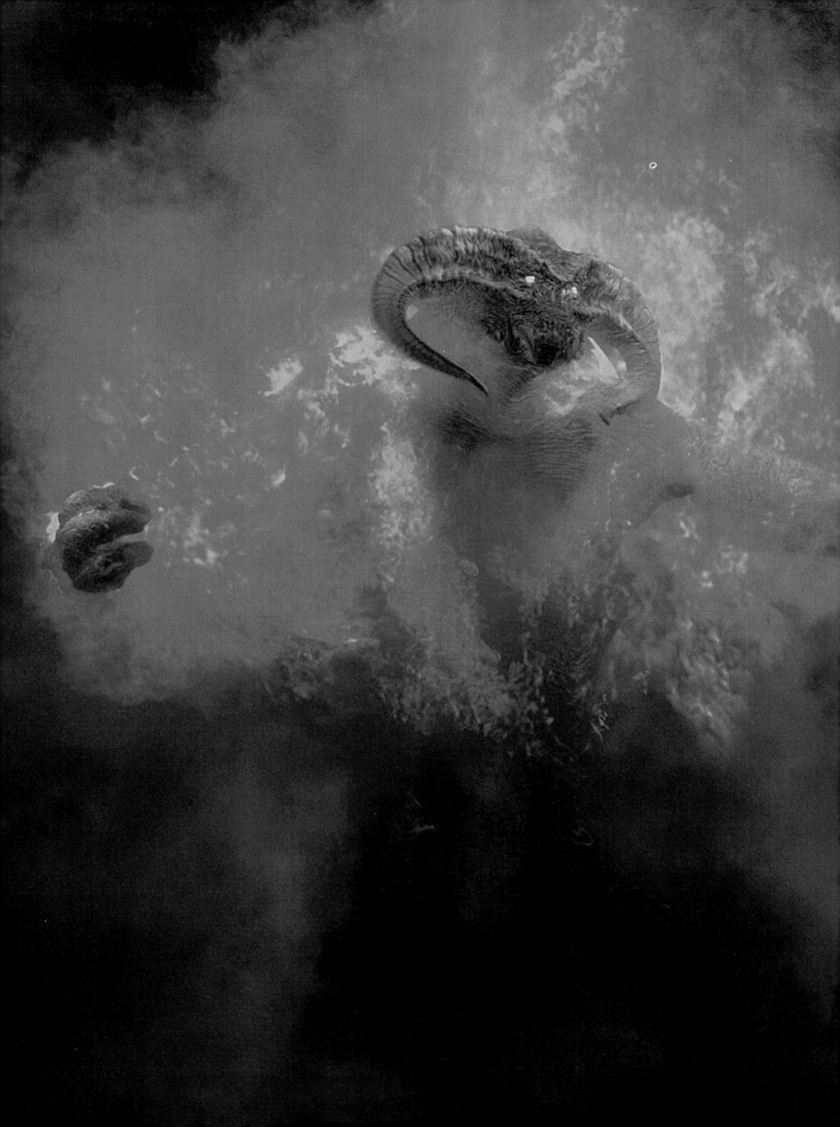

THE KINGDOM OF ROHAN

To the north of Gondor lies the realm of Rohan, known by its people as the Riddermark. It is bordered to the west by the Gap and Fords of Isen (beyond which lies the wizard Saruman's stronghold of Isengard), by the River Limlight in the north, by the Entwash which flows out of Fangorn Forest in the east; and by the White Mountains in the south. The wide, grassy plains of the Riddermark stretch for league upon league in all directions like a great green ocean, and it is here that for generations the people of Rohan — the Rohirrim — have bred the magnificent horses for which they are famed throughout Middle-earth, earning them the title of 'the Horse-lords'.

THE ROHIRRIM

"Where now the horse and the rider? Where is the horn that was blowing?

Where is the helm and the hauberk, and the bright hair flowing?

Where is the hand on the harpstring, and the red fire glowing?

Where is the spring and the harvest and the tall corn growing?

They have passed like rain on the mountain, like a wind in the meadow;

The days have gone down in the West behind the hills into shadow."

The Horse-lords of Rohan are a proud and ancient people of the race of Men. Stern-faced and handsome they are, brave and generous of spirit. They write no books, but they make many songs celebrating their deeds in battle, or the fine horses they breed. The Riders of Rohan, mounted on their fine Riddermark horses, wear burnished skirts of mail to their knees, and carry tall spears of ash and painted shields slung at their backs. They wear their flaxen hair long and in braids, under their decorated helms. Tall and fierce, they are well versed in the arts of war, as needs must, for ever since winning their lands they have had to defend them on every border — from raids by Orcs and Uruk-hai (who have lately encroached as far as the Fords of Isen, there mortally wounding King Théoden's heir Théodred); from the sea-pirates of Umbar in the south, from the Wild Men and Dunlendings whom they long ago drove into the hill country; and, most disturbingly, from Mordor.

And while they are not yet openly at war with Mordor, they feel the chill of its shadow creeping ever westwards, which makes them wary of all strangers: so when Aragorn, Legolas and Gimli traverse their lands in search of their missing companions, they may not meet with the welcome they expect.

KING THÉODEN

"Théoden no longer recognizes friend from foe ... not even his own kin"

Once a great warrior-king of the proud Rohirrim, the Horse-lords of Rohan, and much beloved by his people, now Théoden sits slumped on his throne in the feast-hall of Meduseld, a man broken in spirit, weighed down by what appears to be premature age and feebleness. In his youth he was tall and proud, strong and stern, as is the nature of the Men of the Riddermark, but tragedy visited his house, striking first his wife, Elfhild, who was lost in childbirth, bearing him his only son, Théodred; then his sister's husband fell to Orcs and his wife, Théoden's beloved younger sister Théodwyn, sickened and died of grief, leaving behind two orphans, Éomer and Éowyn. These two children Théoden should have cared for as a father, but he was bowed down by his losses.

Then the wizard, Saruman, whose lands border those of Rohan, saw his opportunity and engaged the services of a sneaking spy — Gríma, son of Gálmód — known as 'Wormtongue'. For years Gríma has wormed his way into the King's mind, filling it with evil counsel, preparing the way for Saruman to take over the land of Rohan. The wizard's army of Uruk-hai and Orcs encroach ever further into the Riddermark; yet all the while Théoden has sunk further into despair and torpor, unable to take action against these incursions, or even to recognize the dangers. When his sister-son, Éomer, warned his king against Gríma, he became angry with the lad and banished him, to Wormtongue's great satisfaction.

War is advancing upon the peoples of the Riddermark. Mordor's influence creeps ever closer, and Wild Men and Dunlendings, Orcs and Uruk-hai are invading from the west, killing all in their path. Rohan needs its king now more than ever in its history: Théoden of the Rohirrim must be raised from his stupor and once more take up arms and lead his people in battle against the forces of evil, or all will be lost.

EDORAS

"Golden, too, are the posts of its doors"

The chief settlement of the Riddermark is Edoras, the Courts of Rohan, situated on top of a rocky outcrop in the lee of the White Mountains, its circumference protected by a mighty wall and wooden palisade. King Théoden, Lord of Rohan, resides there in Meduseld, the Golden Hall, the high-house of the kingdom, a sumptuous feasting hall thatched as if with gold, its pillars and beams all carved in the complex and beautiful style of the Rohirrim, incorporating a myriad of twining, gripping beasts and horse motifs to mark the great love and respect the Horse-Lords have for their noble animals.

GRÍMA WORMTONGUE

"You were once a man of Rohan..."

Gríma, son of Gálmód, close counsellor to King Théoden of Rohan, is a pale, stooped, cringing man who dresses always in black robes. He is known by all but the King as 'Wormtongue' — for all but the Lord of Rohan see him for what he is — a poisonous viper in the nest of Edoras. Day by day he has poured treacherous words into Théoden's ear, sapping his will and the clear sight by which a king must govern; isolating him from all good influences. The death of Théodred, the King's son, brought home to be tended for the wounds he sustained at the Fords of Isen, may also lie at Gríma's hand. He has even taken Herugrim, the King's sword and the symbol of his power, into his own keeping, and has turned Théoden against all those who might urge the King to war — in particular his nephew, Éomer, Third Marshal of the Mark.

For Gríma is the spy of the wizard Saruman the White, master of neighbouring Isengard, planted in the court of the King in order to weaken him and bring him down. Saruman wishes to subvert the rule of Rohan and he has promised his spy a special prize when at last the realm of the Horse-lords lies within his power: possession of the beautiful Lady Éowyn.

*"Too long have you watched her under your eyelids
and haunted her steps"*

ÉOMER

"We welcomed guests kindly in the better days,
but in these times the unbidden stranger finds us swift and hard"

As Aragorn, Legolas and Gimli pursue the band of Uruk-hai who captured and bore away their hobbit companions, Merry and Pippin, they enter the lands of the Riddermark. There, they come upon a group of fierce horsemen, Riders of Rohan. Their captain is a tall, stern man, steel-helmed, mail-shirted and well-armed. His name is Éomer, son of Éomund, and he is the Third Marshal of the Riddermark, nephew to Théoden, King of Rohan. With his men, and against the orders of his lord — who has fallen prey to the evil counsels of Gríma Wormtongue — he is out hunting Orcs; and any others who may be enemies to the kingdom.

"'I serve only the Lord of the Mark, Théoden King, son of Thengel'"

Gríma, the spy, has been poisoning the mind of the King against those who would serve him honestly, and as a result he has persuaded Théoden to regard his brave and faithful nephew as a dangerous traitor who would stir up conflict for his own advancement.

"Put your trust in Éomer,
rather than a man of crooked mind"

But the scales could fall from the Lord of the Mark's eyes, if he is released from the treacher-ous bewitchment that has bound him for so long. With enemies closing in from all sides, King Théoden must realize that Éomer — a fine soldier, valiant warrior and a man of wisdom and understanding — is exactly the kind of hero the Kingdom of Rohan seeks in its hour of need.

ÉOWYN

"You are the daughter of kings, a shield maiden of Rohan..."

Éowyn, Lady of Rohan, is the daughter of Éomund, Marshal of the Mark, who was lost to Orc-attack when she was only a girl, and King Théoden's sister, Théodwyn, who succumbed to grief at the loss of her husband. King Théoden brought Éowyn and her elder brother Éomer to Edoras, and there raised them as his own, until he fell beneath the sinister influence of Gríma Wormtongue and became old, infirm and befuddled before his time.

"Fair and cold, like a morning of pale spring..."

The people of Rohan are by nature fierce and grave, but Éowyn's upbringing has weighed heavily upon her: there has been little care-free pleasure in her life, and laughter does not come easily to her. Willowy and fair, with her pale skin and her long hair like a river of gold she is undeniably beautiful, but she has a chilly aspect and a regard as stern as steel. Nevertheless, Gríma Wormtongue is captivated by Éowyn; and his master, the wizard Saruman, has promised her to him when the realm of Rohan falls beneath his power. But when Éowyn sets her eyes upon the Lord Aragorn, heir of kings, her heart is lost; albeit his is given to Arwen Evenstar, Lady of Rivendell.

The Lady of Rohan wears an ancient sword, and she has as much skill in its use as any man. Soon she will have the need to use it.

HORSES OF THE RIDDERMARK

The horses that have for generations been bred by the Men of Rohan are big and strong and clean-limbed, with coats that glisten and long, flowing manes and tails. Swift and powerful, they can run like the wind. Great herds of them roamed the eastern part of the Riddermark, watched over by nomadic herdsmen, but lately because of the growing threat from Mordor, they have been withdrawn into the interior for safety.

SHADOWFAX

Chief of the Mearas, the greatest horses of Rohan and 'lord of all horses', Shadowfax knows the speech of Men and has the power to outrun even the horses of the Nazgûl. He is so named because his coat is silver-grey.

BREGO

"Stille nu, faeste... Hwaet nemnath the?"

Quiet now, steady... What do they call you?

A fine bay stallion survived the skirmish at the Fords of Isen where his rider, the Lord Théodred, was wounded, and returned to the stables at Edoras. Since then he has been wild and will suffer no one to approach him until Aragorn, son of Arathorn, comes to him and quiets him in his own language of Rohirric and that of the Elves, for Aragorn was raised for a time in Rivendell. The horse is called Brego, in honour of the second King of Rohan, and a strong bond will be forged between the horse and his new rider; a bond that will serve Aragorn well when Orcs attack the company on the road to Dunharrow.

THE HARROWING OF ROHAN

"He has taken Orcs into his service, and Wolf-riders, and evil Men, and he has closed the Gap against us, so that we are likely to be beset both east and west"

Once, the grasslands of Rohan rolled across the plains like a great, green sea, and the Horse-lords kept their herds and studs in the east of the realm, their herdsmen living a peaceful, nomadic existence, moving from grazing ground to grazing ground and from village to village; but since Mordor's shadow has lengthened into that quarter the land there now lies empty, brooding under an ominous silence, a silence that does not seem to be the quiet of peace.

From the west comes another threat, from beyond the Gap of Rohan, the pass that lies between the White Mountains and the Misty Mountains and acts as a gateway into the kingdom. The Gap is guarded by the fortress at Isengard, dwelling-place of Saruman the White, who has for long professed himself a friend to the Rohirrim and their king. But Orcs and Uruk-hai have increasingly been making forays into Rohan through the Gap. And not just Orcs: for his own purposes, it seems, Saruman has exhorted the ancient enemies of Rohan — the Wild Men and the Dunlendings, who long ago were driven off their land and into the hills — to rise up and join with his own vile army.

"They do not come to destroy Rohan's crops or villages – they come to destroy its people ...down to the last child."

The land of Rohan is being harrowed: settlements are ravaged, the buildings put to the torch; men, women and children cut down as they flee. Rohirrim warriors try to hold back these evil forces and defend their people, but they are cruelly outnumbered. Théodred, son of Théoden, was injured in battle at the Fords of Isen, and many of his men lost their lives; now the survivors of such conflicts and thousands of refugees from burned villages must flee toward Dunharrow, and seek safe haven in the impregnable stronghold of Helm's Deep.

WARG-RIDERS

During the Third Age of Middle-earth, the Wargs of Rhovanion made an alliance with the Orcs of the Misty Mountains. When Saruman the White began to draw together his army from the many enemies of the Free Peoples of Middle-earth, the Wargs and their Orc allies came down from the mountains the further to strengthen the wizard's forces.

Because of the great size of the wolf-like Wargs – at least as big as the horses of Rohan – the Orcs used them to ride them into battle. The Wargs are extremely vicious and efficient hunters, able to cover vast distances tirelessly in their search for prey. Because of this, they represent a huge threat to any who would cross the plains of Rohan undefended.

ARWEN'S CHOICE

"I looked into your future, and I saw death."

Thousands of years before the events that are now unfolding, an Elven maiden and a mortal man came together, fell in love and pledged their troth, in desperate times, in defiance of their different races and against all the odds. Their names were Beren and Lúthien.

Beren was a hero among men, a scion of the house of Barahir. One day, in the forest of Neldoreth he saw a figure dancing, and so beautiful was she that he was struck dumb. She was Lúthien, daughter of Thingol of the eternal race of Elves; and from that moment Beren lost his heart; although he knew that if she were to forsake her people to be with him, she must also forsake her immortality.

In the Third Age of Middle-earth, another mortal man chanced on an Elven maiden in the woods at Rivendell, and she was in her own time of all living things the most fair; for she was Arwen, the descendant of Lúthien. Like Beren, the man who spied her there was doomed to love from the first moment he saw her; this was Aragorn, son of Arathorn, and he was descended from Beren's line,

as token of which he wore the Ring of Barahir. Aragorn did not know that this maid was the daughter of Elrond who had raised him in Rivendell since he was a child, for during all the years in which Aragorn had been in Rivendell, Arwen had been in Lothlórien with the Lady Galadriel, her mother's mother.

Although he perceived the love which lay between Aragorn and Arwen, the Lord Elrond would not permit their betrothal: for his daughter was fated to leave the world of men and pass with him into the Undying Lands, there to live forever as an immortal; while Aragorn's shoulders were to bear another destiny entirely: to fight the forces of evil in the War of the Ring and to live out his short span as a mortal man in Middle-earth.

The love between Aragorn and Arwen parallels the kinship between Men and Elves; both, at this time in the Third Age, with the Shadow falling over all, rest on a knife-edge.

HELM'S DEEP

Helm's Deep, named for Helm Hammerhand, the hero of ancient wars who made his refuge there, lies in a gorge that winds its way below three-peaked Thrihyrne in the northern White Mountains. It has long been the defensive centre of the Westfold and the kings of Rohan have over the ages constructed a vast and seemingly impregnable system of fortification in the gorge, including defensive walls and keeps.

"No army has ever breached the Deeping Wall nor set foot inside the Hornburg.

Not while Men of Rohan defend it..."

The entrance to the Deep is commanded by Helm's Gate, a tall wooden gate now rotting with age and, upon a great spur of rock, the towering structure of the Hornburg, a massive-walled keep said to have been built by the hands of giants in the days of the sea-kings of Gondor. From the keep to the mouth of Helm's Gate runs the Deeping Wall, a great fortified wall, wide enough to enable four men at once to stand abreast the top, shielded by its tall parapet and reached by stairs running down from the outer court of the Hornburg. Three flights of steps lead up to the wall from the Deep behind, but the outer surface is smooth and unscaleable. Beneath the Wall lies Helm's Dike, a vast defensive earthwork a mile or more long, cut through only by a stream which runs through a deep culvert.

"Saruman's arm will have grown long indeed if he thinks he can reach us here"

Beneath Helm's Deep lie the Glittering Caves of Aglarond, a spectacular cavern system which is truly one of Middle-earth's natural wonders, and has proved in times past to be a safe haven when the Kingdom of Rohan is under attack.

PREPARING FOR BATTLE

Massively outnumbered by a horde of ten thousand Orcs and Uruk-hai marching on the gorge from Isengard, the remaining members of the Fellowship and their comrades must prepare for the onslaught of the enemy by donning armour and making ready their weapons. Even though Helm's Deep has proved impregnable in past conflicts, its gates are now rotting and its defenders are few. The odds against the people of Rohan and its allies are appalling: no matter how valiantly they fight, they can surely never triumph.

"I am of the world of Men and these are my people: I will die as one of them..."

Over his tunic, Aragorn puts on a short-sleeved shirt of heavy chainmail and protects his fore-arms with the tooled leather vambraces once worn by Boromir of Gondor. His sword is keen-edged. Legolas, prince of the Mirkwood Elves, dons armour for the first time in his life. He carries two lethal white knives at his belt, his great Galadhrim longbow and the peacock-decorated quiver of arrows given to him by the Lady Galadriel in Lothlórien. The Dwarf-warrior,

Gimli, son of Glóin remains battle-dressed in his own leather armour and impressive iron helmet, and carries five fearsome battle-axes.

"Arise now, arise, Riders of Théoden!

Dire deeds awake, dark is it eastward.

Let horse be bridled, horn be sounded!

Forth, Eorlingas!"

King Théoden of Rohan is arrayed in full Rohirrim wargear, including a mighty helmet, engraved breastplate and mailshirt. He carries his greatsword Herugrim. Beside him, the Royal Guard of Rohan, led by Gamling, are similarly arrayed.

Just a few hundred refugees from the settlements that have been harrowed by Orcs and Wildmen throughout Rohan have made it through to Helm's Deep. These few will be kitted out for battle in the Hornburg armoury. They are a motley bunch of old men and untested boys; but all are ready to fight to the death to defend their kingdom, even though they are vastly outnumbered and their defence appears doomed.

Down in the Glittering Caves the women and the children take refuge, where they will be defended by Éowyn, shield-maiden of Rohan.

The sky is darkening: a storm is brewing...

ELVES AND MEN

"The world is changing. I feel it in the water. I feel it in the earth and I smell it in the air.

Our time here is over..."

The Elves last fought alongside Men to combat the forces of evil at the Battle of Dagorlad, which brought about the downfall of Sauron and ended the Second Age. Now, in the Third Age, Sauron has steadily rebuilt his strength and his armies, while the Elves have dwindled, both in number and in their influence upon the peoples of Middle-earth. In increasing numbers, they have made the decision to pass out of this war-torn, sorrowful world over the Sea and into the Undying Lands, where they may enjoy their immortality in peace and bliss.

"In days of old our people stood beside the King of Gondor..."

Acknowledgments

My warmest thanks to the following for their help and support in the making of this book:

Jeremy Bennett, Hannah Bianchini, Jan Blenkin, Philippa Boyens, David Brawn, Terence Caven, Claire Cooper, John Howe, David Imhoff, Peter Jackson, Alan Lee, Erin O'Donnell, Mark Ordesky, Barry Osborne, Chris Smith, Fran Walsh

and particularily to Viggo Mortensen for taking time and care to craft his fine introduction.

HarperCollins*Publishers*
77–85 Fulham Palace Road,
Hammersmith, London W6 8JB
www.tolkien.co.uk

Published by HarperCollins*Publishers* 2002
1 3 5 7 9 8 6 4 2

Text © Jude Fisher 2002

Photographs, Stills, Film Script Excerpts, Film Logos
© 2002 New Line Productions, Inc. All Rights Reserved.

Compilation © HarperCollins*Publishers* 2002

'The Lord of the Rings', 'The Two Towers' and the
characters and the places therein, ™ The Saul Zaentz Company d/b/a
Tolkien Enterprises under license to New Line Productions, Inc.
All Rights Reserved.

'Tolkien' ® is a trademark of The J.R.R. Tolkien Estate Limited.

The Lord of the Rings: The Two Towers Visual Companion
is a companion to the film *The Two Towers* and it is not
published with the approval of the Estate of the late J.R.R. Tolkien.
Dialogue quotations are from the film, not the novel.

The Lord of the Rings and its constituent volumes, *The Fellowship
of the Ring, The Two Towers* and *The Return of the King*,
are published by HarperCollins*Publishers* under licence from
The Trustees of The J.R.R. Tolkien 1967 Settlement.

Jude Fisher asserts the moral right to
be identified as the author of this work

Photographs: Pierre Vinet & Chris Coad
Editor: Chris Smith
Design: Terence Caven
Production: Arjen Jansen

A catalogue record for this book
is available from the British Library

ISBN 0 00 711625 X

Set in Slimbach

Printed and bound in Belgium by Proost NV, Turnhout